The Usborne
Picture
Dictionary

Illustrated by MIGUEL SANCHEZ

Written by
CAROLINE YOUNG

Edited by
FELICITY BROOKS

Designed by
KIRSTY TIZZARD

All about dictionaries

Dictionaries are amazing books. They tell you what words mean, how to use them and how they are spelled. They are a little different than other books, too. Here's how:

1 The words in a dictionary are in the same order as the alphabet. This means that ones that begin with A come first, then ones that begin with B, all the way through to Z.

2 Instead of reading across each page, as you do when you read other kinds of books, with a dictionary you read

down

the page, in columns.

3 In this dictionary, pictures and captions tell you more about what each word means and how it can be used.

So, what can I see on the pages?

This word shows the first word on the page.

This word shows the last word on the page.

These are the words you can look up. They are in alphabetical order.

This writing explains what the word means.

You can find out what these words in parentheses mean on pages 118 to 120.

If the same word appears twice with little numbers, it shows that the word can be used in very different ways.

This letter shows you the first letter of all the words on this page.

These numbers show that this word has more than one meaning.

This writing shows you how you could use the word.

Finding a word

To find a word in this dictionary, follow the four steps under this picture. It's really easy when you get used to it.

I need to find the word "bear."

1

Think of the letter the word starts with. "bear" starts with "b," for example.

2

Now look through the dictionary until you find the pages where all the words begin with "b."

3

Think of the second letter of your word. For "bear," it's an "e," so look for words that start with "be."

4

Now look down all the "be" words after "beach" until you find "bear."

The first "be" word is "beach." Can you see it?

Aa

act
pretend to be another person in a play or movie

Jada loves acting.

add
1 combine two numbers

Can you add 4 and 6?

2 put or mix things together

Dad adds milk to his tea.

address
words and numbers that show you where someone lives

This is Katie's address.

Katie Flowers
72 Pansy Lane
Gardenstown
TX 56088

adult
someone who is a grown-up

My mom is an adult.

afraid
If you are afraid of something, it scares you.

Lucas is afraid of spiders.

after
Something that happens after something else happens later than it.

The night comes after the day.

afternoon
the part of the day after the morning

4 o'clock in the afternoon

age
how old you are

Can you guess my age?

air
what we all breathe

airport
somewhere planes take off and land

alone
If you are alone, you are not with anyone else.

Joseph is alone on the seesaw.

alphabet
all the letters you need to make words

There are 26 letters in this alphabet.

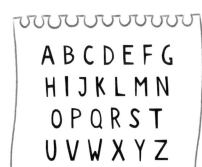

ABCDEFG
HIJKLMN
OPQRST
UVWXYZ

ambulance
a special van that carries people who are sick or hurt

This ambulance is going to the hospital.

amount
how much there is of something

a small amount of money

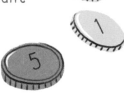

angel
a messenger sent from heaven

angry
If you are angry, you feel upset and want to shout.

animal
something that lives, moves and breathes

An aardvark is an animal.

ankle
the bony part of your body between your leg and your foot

app
a small computer program that helps you do things

I have eight apps on my phone.

apple
a fruit with red, green or yellow skin

a red apple

a
b
c
d
e
f
g
h
i
j
k
l
m
n
o
p
q
r
s
t
u
v
w
x
y
z

a b c d e f g h i j k l m n o p q r s t u v w x y z

arm
the long part of your body between your shoulder and hand

arrive
get to where you are going

Gran has arrived!

artist
someone who makes art

ask
1 say you want to know something

Can I ask you a question?

Sure! Ask me anything!

art
Art is something that is made to be beautiful, or to show feelings and ideas. There are lots of different kinds of art.

painting

drama   dance

music

2 say you want something

Ben is asking for some water.

Can I have a glass of water, please?

asleep
If you are asleep, you are not awake. You are sleeping.

Sara is asleep.

astronaut
someone who goes into space

Bb

baby (babies)

a very young child

This baby is smiling.

back¹

the part of your body between your neck and bottom

I really need to scratch my back!

back²

The back of something is furthest from the front.

I'm at the back of the line.

bad (worse, worst)

1 not good

That's a very bad haircut.

2 not nice to eat

These strawberries are bad.

bag

something you carry things in

bake

cook food such as bread and cakes in an oven

baker

someone who makes and sells bread and cakes

Mr. Liebowicz is an amazing baker.

balance

keep your body or something steady so it does not fall

It's tricky to balance like this.

ballet

a kind of dance

ballet shoes

balloon

a rubber or plastic bag you can fill with air

7

a b c d e f g h i j k l m n o p q r s t u v w x y z

a
b
c
d
e
f
g
h
i
j
k
l
m
n
o
p
q
r
s
t
u
v
w
x
y
z

banana

a long, curved fruit with thick yellow skin

band

a group of people who play music together

bank¹

a place where people keep their money

bank²

the land beside a stream or river

Ducks build nests on the banks of rivers.

bar

a block of something

a bar of solid gold

bare

If something is not covered with anything, it is bare.

a bare branch

bark¹

the hard skin that covers a tree trunk

bark²

a loud sound dogs make

Dogs don't shout, they bark.

barn

a big building on a farm for keeping things in

Farmer Kirsty keeps a tractor in this barn.

base

the bottom part of something

The base of this vase is blue.

basket

something that you can keep and carry things in

bat¹

a small, furry animal that flies at night

bat²

a kind of stick you use to hit a ball

a baseball bat

bathtub

something you fill with water and sit in to wash your body

a bathtub full of bubbles

beach

the land beside the sea or a lake covered with sand or small stones

a sandy beach

beak

the hard outside part of a bird's mouth

Toucans have big, bright beaks.

bean

a long, thin vegetable or the seeds inside it

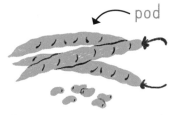

pod

Beans grow in a pod.

bear

a big wild animal with thick fur and sharp claws

beard

hair that grows on someone's chin

Mario has a big beard.

beautiful

lovely to look at, listen to or smell

a beautiful bunch of flowers

In English, there are lots of words that mean "beautiful."

Can you think of any more?

lovely

pretty

nice

bed

something you lie on to rest or go to sleep

a b c d e f g h i j k l m n o p q r s t u v w x y z

9

a
b
c
d
e
f
g
h
i
j
k
l
m
n
o
p
q
r
s
t
u
v
w
x
y
z

bedroom
a room you sleep in

Rhian has a pretty bedroom.

bee
a yellow and black insect that makes honey

beetle
an insect with a hard, shiny cover over its wings

before
Something that happens before something else happens first.

Meg walks the dog before school.

begin
start something

This is where you begin this book.

behind
Something that is behind something else is at the back of it.

The bike is behind the car.

belong
If something belongs to you, it is yours.

This ball belongs to me.

below
Something that is below something else is lower than it.

The cups are below the bowls.

belt
a strip of plastic, cloth or leather that you wear around your stomach

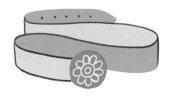

a green belt

beside
Something that is beside something is next to it.

Grandpa is sitting beside the fire.

between

Something that is between two things is in the middle of them.

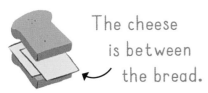

The cheese is between the bread.

bib

something that babies wear around their necks to keep their clothes clean

bicycle

something with two wheels that you can ride

bird

an animal with feathers, wings and a beak

KRAAKK!

Seagulls are noisy birds.

birthday

the date you were born

HAPPY BIRTHDAY!

bite (bit, bitten)

cut into food with your teeth

big

large; not small

In English, there are lots of words that mean big. Here are some of them. Can you think of any more?

HUGE   MASSIVE
ENORMOUS

Am I big?

You are gigantic!

blanket

a soft cover on a bed

Mom made this beautiful blanket.

blog

a place online where people write about things

MY FOOTBALL BLOG

blow (blew, blown)

1 make air come out of your mouth

Pip is blowing up the balloon.

2 When the wind blows, it moves air around.

The wind blows the seeds away.

a
b
c
d
e
f
g
h
i
j
k
l
m
n
o
p
q
r
s
t
u
v
w
x
y
z

a
b
c
d
e
f
g
h
i
j
k
l
m
n
o
p
q
r
s
t
u
v
w
x
y
z

boat

something that carries people and things across water

canoe

speedboat

rowboat

body (bodies)

Your body is every part of you.

I love to move my body!

bone

one of the hard, white parts inside your body

There are 27 bones in a hand.

book

something you read, with pages fixed inside a cover

boot

a kind of tall shoe that covers your foot and your ankle

a pair of boots

bottle

a container for holding liquid, usually made of plastic, glass or metal

bottom¹

the part of your body you sit on

bottom²

the lowest part of something

There's a hole in the bottom of my bag!

bowl

a round, deep plate for holding food

box

a container for keeping things in, often made of cardboard or wood

boy
a child who is not a girl

boy   man

branch
the part of a tree that leaves grow on

This branch is covered with leaves.

brave
If you are brave, you are not afraid.

Alfie was very brave at the hospital.

bread
a kind of food made from flour and baked in an oven

break¹ (broke, broken)
make something split into pieces or stop working

This toy is broken.

break²
a pause between activities, or a short vacation

Mom is having a break.

breakfast
the first meal you eat each day

breathe
bring air into your nose or mouth and then let it out again

bridge
something built over a road, river or railway so that people can get across

Tower Bridge, London

bright
Something bright is colorful and easy to see.

Uncle Jim's sweater is VERY bright.

bring
(brought, brought)
take something or someone with you

Tom brought his sister to the park.

a b c d e f g h i j k l m n o p q r s t u v w x y z

a
b
c
d
e
f
g
h
i
j
k
l
m
n
o
p
q
r
s
t
u
v
w
x
y
z

brush

something you use to clean your teeth, smooth your hair, paint or sweep

paintbrush

hairbrush

bubble

a ball of gas inside a liquid

Jed blew a big bubble.

bucket

something you can carry things in

Cal carries beach toys in her bucket.

bug

an insect or very small animal

shieldbug

earwig

build (built, built)

make something by putting things together

Lily has built a tower.

building

somewhere with walls and a roof

a tall building

bully (bullies)

someone who hurts or is unkind to other people

bump

knock something by mistake

Tina has bumped her knee.

Ouch!

burger

a thin circle of chopped up food, usually inside a bun

burn

1 damage or hurt something with heat or fire

I've burned my toast!

2 be on fire

Dry logs burn better than wet ones.

bus

a big thing on wheels that can carry a lot of people

We go to school by bus.

bush

a big plant with lots of leaves and branches

a rose bush

busy

If you are busy, you have lots of things to do.

Mr. Kumar is very busy.

butcher

someone who prepares and sells meat

butter

a soft, yellow food made from milk

butterfly
(butterflies)

an insect with four large wings

button

a small, round thing for fastening clothes

buy
(bought, bought)

give money for something so you can have it

I'd like to buy three bananas.

15

a
b
c
d
e
f
g
h
i
j
k
l
m
n
o
p
q
r
s
t
u
v
w
x
y
z

Cc

a b c d e f g h i j k l m n o p q r s t u v w x y z

café

somewhere you can buy and eat snacks and drinks

cage

a box or room with bars that keeps animals safe

cake

sweet food usually made from sugar, flour, eggs and butter

calf (calves)

a young cow

call

shout for someone or an animal to come to you

Wags, come here!

calm

If someone or something is calm, they are quiet or still.

Jon's kitten is very calm.

camel

a large animal that has one or two humps and lives in a desert

camera

something you use to take photographs

camp

sleep in a tent

Tanya likes to camp in the mountains.

candle

a stick of wax with a string through the middle that burns

There are four candles on this cake.

cap

a soft hat with a part at the front to shade your eyes

a baseball cap

car

a machine that people drive on roads. It usually has four wheels.

This car is very full.

card

something you send to someone at a special time

a birthday card

HAPPY BIRTHDAY!

carpet

a thick, soft covering on a floor

carrot

a long, crunchy orange vegetable

carry

pick someone or something up and take them somewhere

Freya is carrying Bobby on her back.

castle

a big, strong building with high stone walls

cat

a small, furry animal that people often keep as a pet

catch
(caught, caught)

1 get hold of something that is moving

Dayan has caught a fish in his net.

2 get on a bus, plane or train

I need to catch that bus!

caterpillar

a small, long animal that turns into a butterfly or moth

a b c d e f g h i j k l m n o p q r s t u v w x y z

a
b
c
d
e
f
g
h
i
j
k
l
m
n
o
p
q
r
s
t
u
v
w
x
y
z

cauliflower

a round vegetable with a white middle and green leaves

cave

a big hole in a cliff or mountain, or under the ground

Wow, it's dark in this cave!

center

the middle of something

The toys are in the center

cereal

food that you eat with milk, usually for breakfast

chair

a seat that one person can sit on

a red chair

chalk

soft white or colored sticks that you can draw or write with

change

make something different from the way it was

Molly changed the color of her hair.

charge

plug a phone in so that it will keep working

chase

run after someone or something

Reggie likes to chase his toy mouse.

SQUEAK
SQUEAK

cheap

not costing too much money

Things in this store are very cheap.

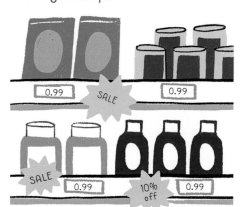

cheese
a food made from milk

There are lots of kinds of cheese.

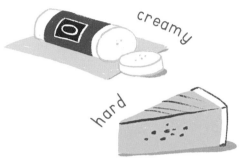
creamy
hard

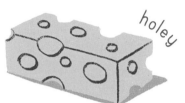
holey

chef
someone who cooks food in a restaurant

Ella is a chef.

cherry (cherries)
a small, round red fruit with a hard pit in the center

chest¹
the front part of your body between your shoulders

chest²
a big strong box with a lid

a treasure chest

chick
a very young bird

chicken
1 (also called a hen) a bird that farmers keep for eggs and meat

2 the meat that comes from a chicken

child (children)
a young person

three children

chin
the part of your face below your mouth

Lara has a freckle on her chin.

chocolate
a sweet and sugary food

a b c d e f g h i j k l m n o p q r s t u v w x y z

choose – close

a b c d e f g h i j k l m n o p q r s t u v w x y z

choose
(chose, chosen)

decide what you want

Which one should I choose?

chop

cut something up into smaller pieces

city (cities)

a very big place where lots of people live and work

This city is called Paris.

class

a group of people who learn together

Miss West's Class

classroom

a room where teachers teach lessons

Our classroom is very colorful.

clean[1]

get rid of dirt

Mr. Arnold cleans our school.

clean[2]

without any dirt on it

My bike is clean now.

climb

step or pull yourself up something

Squirrels climb trees.

clock

something that shows you the time

close[1]

shut something
(You say "kloze.")

Close the door, please. I'm freezing!

close[2]

not far from; near
(You say "klose.")

Our house is close
to the park.

our house

clothes

things you wear

cloud

white or gray shapes
that float in the sky

Clouds are full of tiny
drops of water.

coat

something you
wear to keep
you warm
and dry

coconut

a round fruit with a
hard, brown, hairy shell

coffee

a hot, brown drink
made from roasted
coffee beans

coin

a small, round piece
of metal money

cold[1]

not hot or warm
When it's very cold,
it sometimes snows.

In English, there are lots
of words that mean cold.
Here are a few.

chilly   icy

freezing

Can you
think of
any more?

cold[2]

an illness that makes
you cough and sneeze

ACHOO

color

Red, blue and green
are all colors.

red   blue   green

a b c d e f g h i j k l m n o p q r s t u v w x y z

a
b
c
d
e
f
g
h
i
j
k
l
m
n
o
p
q
r
s
t
u
v
w
x
y
z

comb

something you can use to keep hair neat and free from tangles

come (came, came)

move towards something or someone

The tram is coming!

computer

a machine you use to write and send messages and to check and store information

cook¹

prepare food so that it is ready to eat

Uncle Dan is cooking dinner.

cook²

someone who makes meals

HanJie is a very good cook.

copy

do the same thing as someone else

The kitten is copying her mother.

country¹ (countries)

a part of the world with its own people, languages and laws

This country is called Italy.

country²

the land outside towns and cities

We like walking in the country.

cow

a big animal that farmers keep for milk or meat

crab

a sea creature with a hard shell, eight legs and two claws

crane

a tall, powerful machine for lifting heavy things

crash
bang into something suddenly and loudly

Milo's toy car crashed into the flowerpot.

crayon
a colored pencil or a pencil made from wax

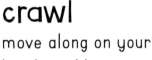

crawl
move along on your hands and knees

creep (crept, crept)
move very quietly and slowly

The tiger is creeping through the grass.

crocodile
a big animal with sharp teeth and a long tail

cross
go from one side to the other

Nareen is crossing the road.

crown
a special gold or silver hat that a king or queen wears

cry (cried, cried)
When you cry, tears fall from your eyes.

cucumber
a long, green vegetable that you eat in salads

cup
something you drink from. A cup usually has a handle.

cut (cut, cut)
divide something into pieces with a knife or scissors

Leah is cutting the paper.

cycle
ride a bicycle

I cycle to school with my brother.

a b c d e f g h i j k l m n o p q r s t u v w x y z

23

Dd

dance
move your body
to music

dangerous
If something is dangerous,
it could hurt or kill you.

That looks
dangerous.

dark
1 If it is dark, there is no
light or hardly any light.

It's dark at night.

2 If a color is dark,
it is not pale or light.

light green   dark green

date
the day and month
something happens

the date of
the party

OCTOBER
16th

day
1 the time when it is
light outside

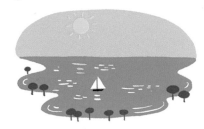

2 the 24 hours
from one
midnight
to the next

dead
If something is dead,
it is not alive anymore.

a dead plant

dear
a word you use before
a name at the beginning
of a letter or email

Dear Uncle Gary,

Thank you for
my present.

decide
make a choice

Laticia can't decide
which book to read.

deep
going down a long way

Dad is digging a deep
hole in the garden.

deer (deer)

a large animal that often lives in woods and forests

desert

a very dry place where it hardly ever rains

different

not the same

two different hats

delicious

tasting really nice

These look delicious!

desk

a table for working on

difficult

not easy to do

I find knitting difficult.

deliver

get something to someone

Aaron delivered Mom's packages.

dictionary (dictionaries)

a book full of words and their meanings

Picture Dictionary

dig (dug, dug)

make a hole in the ground

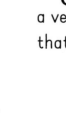

Maisie loves to dig.

dentist

someone who takes care of your teeth and gums

die (died, died)

When something stops living, it dies.

Flowers die without any water.

digger

a very big machine that digs

a b c d e f g h i j k l m n o p q r s t u v w x y z

25

a
b
c
d
e
f
g
h
i
j
k
l
m
n
o
p
q
r
s
t
u
v
w
x
y
z

dinner

the biggest meal you have each day

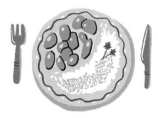

dinosaur

an animal that lived millions of years ago

dirty

covered with mud, food or other things

Libby's soccer clothes are dirty.

disappear

If something disappears, you cannot see it anymore.

The magician made the cards disappear.

dishwasher

a machine that washes plates, bowls, cups and other things

dive (dove *or* dived)

jump into water with your hands and head first

diver

someone who explores underwater

do (did, done)

1 make something happen

Jamal is doing his homework.

2 finish something

I've done it!

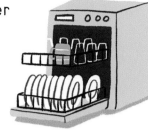

doctor

someone who helps people when they are sick

dog

an animal people keep as a pet, or to work for them

doll

a toy that looks like a small person

dolphin

a very clever animal that lives in the sea

donkey

an animal that looks like a horse with long ears

door

something you use to get into somewhere

down

from a higher place to a lower one

Lola is walking down the stairs.

download

copy something from the internet onto your computer

Zach is downloading a movie.

dragon

in stories, a creature that can breathe fire

draw

(drew, drawn)

make a picture with a pencil, pen or crayon

Evangeline is drawing.

drawing

a picture someone has made with a pencil, pen or crayons

dream

a story that comes into your head while you are sleeping

dress¹

a piece of clothing

Sabrina has a new dress.

dress²

put your clothes on

a b c **d** e f g h i j k l m n o p q r s t u v w x y z

27

a
b
c
d
e
f
g
h
i
j
k
l
m
n
o
p
q
r
s
t
u
v
w
x
y
z

drink¹ (drank, drunk)

swallow water or another liquid

Ellie is drinking a glass of cold water.

drink²

a liquid you swallow

Nana's lemonade is a delicious drink.

drive (drove, driven)

make a car, bus or truck move

Lexi drives a truck at work.

drop¹

let something fall by accident

I've dropped the vase!

drop²

a very small amount of liquid

a drop of water

drum

a musical instrument you hit with sticks or your hands

dry¹ (dried, dried)

take the water off something

Clive is drying the dishes.

dry²

If something is dry, it is not wet or damp.

This towel is dry.

duck

a bird that lives near water and dives and swims

duckling

a very young duck

Ducklings are small and fluffy.

dull

1 boring or not very interesting

This movie is so dull.

2 not bright or shiny

dull   shiny

Ee

eagle
a large bird with sharp claws and a curved beak

ear
one of the parts of your body that you use for hearing

These are my ears.

early
sooner than expected

Finn woke up too early.

Earth[1]
the planet we live on

earth[2]
the stuff that most plants grow in

earth

This flower's roots go down into the earth.

easy
If something is easy, it is not very hard or difficult to do.

cat

"Cat" is an easy word to spell.

eat (ate, eaten)
chew and swallow food

Pandas like to eat bamboo.

edge
the outside part of something

We're walking around the edge of the lake.

egg
a smooth, round or oval case that may have a baby bird, fish, insect or reptile inside it

a
b
c
d
e
f
g
h
i
j
k
l
m
n
o
p
q
r
s
t
u
v
w
x
y
z

elbow

the bony part of your arm where it bends

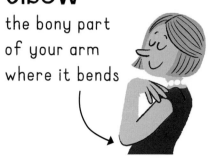

electricity

the power that makes lights, TVs, computers and machines work

How many things can you think of that use electricity?

elephant

a very big, gray animal with a long nose that is called a trunk

trunk

email

a message you send from a phone or computer

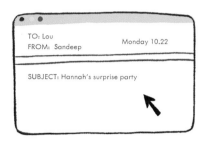

TO: Lou
FROM: Sandeep
Monday 10.22

SUBJECT: Hannah's surprise party

Sandeep is writing an email.

empty

with nothing inside it

an empty box

end

where something finishes

Toby has reached the end of the story.

THE END

enjoy

If you enjoy something, you like doing it.

Wyn enjoys baking.

enormous

very big

an enormous building

There are several words in English for "very big." Here are some of them.

MASSIVE

HUGE

GIANT

Can you think of any more?

entrance
the way in

envelope
a paper or cardboard packet for letters, cards or small packages

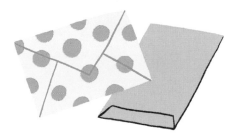

environment
everything that surrounds you

a peaceful environment

equal
the same

These ladybugs have an equal number of spots.

even
If a number is even, you can divide it by 2.

Here, all the even numbers have a circle around them.

evening
the part of the day between the afternoon and the night

The sun sets in the evening.

exit
the way out

Follow the signs for the exit.

expensive
If something is expensive, it costs a lot.

Wow, this skateboard is expensive!

explain
help someone understand something

Our teacher explains things really well.

eye
one of the parts of your body that you use for seeing

I have green eyes.

a b c d e f g h i j k l m n o p q r s t u v w x y z

Ff

face

the front part
of your head

facing

If you are facing someone
or something, you are
looking towards them.

These houses are
facing each other.

fact

something that is true

It is a fact that there
are stars in the sky.

Yes,
that's a
fact!

fairy (fairies)

in stories, a tiny
person with wings
and magical powers

fall (fell, fallen)

suddenly drop to
the ground

These leaves have
fallen on the ground.

far

a long way

That cow is far away.

Mooooo

farm

a place where farmers
keep animals and grow
plants for food

farmer

a person who lives
and works on
a farm

fast

very quick or quickly

Steve is going very fast.

fat

with a big, round body

a fat walrus

feed (fed, fed)

give food to something or someone

Jo feeds her fish every day.

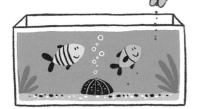

feel (felt, felt)

1 touch something to find out more about it

This towel feels soft.

2 If you feel something, that is how you are at that time.

Chang feels sad.

fence

an outdoor barrier made of metal, wood or wire

few
(fewer, fewest)

not many

a few shells

field

a large piece of land where farmers keep animals or grow plants

a field of wheat

fight
(fought, fought)

try to hurt each other because you do not agree about something

file

1 a stiff plastic or cardboard folder or box for papers

2 a place where things are stored on a computer

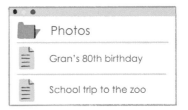

fill

put so much into something that you cannot add any more

Suki is filling the tire with air.

find (found, found)

spot or get something back that was lost

Dhruv is trying to find his other shoe.

a b c d e f g h i j k l m n o p q r s t u v w x y z

33

a
b
c
d
e
f
g
h
i
j
k
l
m
n
o
p
q
r
s
t
u
v
w
x
y
z

finger
one of the long, thin parts at the end of your hand

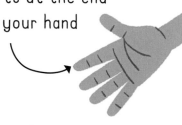

finish
get to the end of something

Jess has nearly finished her dinner.

fire
heat and flames that come from something that is burning

fire engine
a truck that takes firefighters to put out fires

firefighter
someone who puts out fires

first
If you are first, you are ahead of all the others.

Mo won first place.

fish¹ (fish *or* fishes)
an animal that lives underwater

fish²
try to catch fish

Carlos and David are fishing.

fit¹
If clothes fit you, they are the right size.

These shoes fit me perfectly!

fit²
If you are fit, your body is healthy.

Uncle Phil runs every day to keep fit.

fix
1 mend something that was broken

Jack is fixing the broken toy robot.

2 join something to something else

Nina is fixing the shelf to the wall.

flag

a piece of cloth with
a special pattern on it

This flag has a red
dragon on it.

flat

without any lumps
or bumps in it

a flat road

float

1 stay on the surface
of the water
These leaves can float.

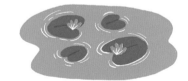

2 stay up in the air

Some balloons
float.

flood

water that covers land
that is usually dry
(You say "flud.")

floor

what you walk on inside
a building

a wooden floor

flour

a powder that you can
use to make bread
and cakes

Most flour
is made from
wheat.

flower

a part of a plant that
is often colorful
and smells nice

fly¹ (flew, flown)

move through the air

Birds can fly.

fly² (flies)

a small insect with
see-through wings

foal

a young horse

fold

bend part of one thing
over another part

This card
is folded
in half.

a b c d e f g h i j k l m n o p q r s t u v w x y z

35

a
b
c
d
e
f
g
h
i
j
k
l
m
n
o
p
q
r
s
t
u
v
w
x
y
z

food

things that people eat

foot (feet)

the part of your body at the end of your leg

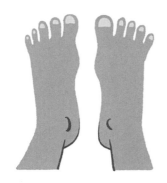

fork

something with points that you use to pick up and eat food

fox

a wild animal that has a long, bushy tail

free

1 If something is free, you do not have to pay for it.

2 allowed to go where you want and do whatever you want

These wild horses are free.

freeze

(froze, frozen)

get very cold and become ice

The pond had frozen in the night.

freezer

something that keeps food very cold so that it lasts longer

fresh

just made or picked

Lisa loves fresh orange juice.

friend

someone you feel close to, and can talk to easily

James and Jacob are best friends.

friendly
kind and warm to other people

Mr. Hart is such a friendly man.

fries
potatoes cut into thin strips and fried in hot oil

frog
an animal that can live in water and on land

front
the part of something that comes first or that you see first

Aunt Mary is in the front of the car.

fruit
sweet food that grows on a plant, bush or tree

grapes

watermelon

kiwi

apricot

fry (fried, fried)
cook in hot oil or butter

Mukesh is frying some onions.

full
with no room in it for anything else

This lunchbox is full.

fun
If something is fun, you really enjoy it.

This is great fun!

funny
If something is funny, it makes you laugh.

This book is so funny!

fur
soft hair that covers some animals and keeps them warm

Polar bears have thick, white fur.

a b c d e f g h i j k l m n o p q r s t u v w x y z

37

Gg

a
b
c
d
e
f
g
h
i
j
k
l
m
n
o
p
q
r
s
t
u
v
w
x
y
z

game
something you play that often has rules or different stages

garage
a building that you keep a car in

garden
land near a house where people can grow flowers or vegetables or just enjoy being outside

gas
something light and invisible in the air

Some gas makes heat when it burns.

gate
a doorway in a wall, fence or hedge

gentle
kind and caring

Nazanin is very gentle with her baby.

gerbil
a small, furry animal that people often keep as a pet

ghost
a person who has died that some people believe they can see

giant
a very tall person who you might find in a story

You're so tall!

gift
something special that you give to someone or that they give to you

To: Mom
From: Jim

giraffe
an animal with a very long neck that lives in Africa

girl

a child who is not a boy

I'm a girl!

I know.

give (gave, given)

let someone have something

Chloe gave Josh her old bike.

glass

1 something hard that you can see through

a window made of glass

2 a drink container that is made of glass

a glass of milk

glasses

something that you can wear on your face to help you see better

a pair of glasses

glove

something you wear to keep your hand warm or protected

glue

something you use to stick things together

go (went, been)

move from one place to another

We're going to the the beach!

goal

You score a goal in some games when you kick, hit or throw a ball into a net.

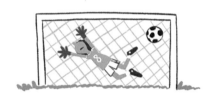

goat

an animal with horns and a short tail

a mountain goat

gold

very expensive yellow-colored metal

a gold ring

a b c d e f g h i j k l m n o p q r s t u v w x y z

a b c d e f **g** h i j k l m n o p q r s t u v w x y z

good (better, best)

1 If something is good, you like it.

This book is very good.

2 A person or animal that behaves well is good.

Juno is such a good dog.

3 If something has been done well, it is good.

Good work, Salman!

7.

10

The word "good" is very useful, but there are other words you could use instead. Here are some of them:

lovely

tasty

kind

Can you think of any more?

goodbye

a word you say when you are leaving or when someone goes away

Goodbye!

goose (geese)

a large farm bird that makes a loud noise

grape

a small green, red or purple fruit that grows in bunches

grapefruit

a large, round fruit with yellow or pink insides that tastes very sour

grass

a plant with lots of thin green leaves that grows in fields and yards.

great

1 very important

Vincent van Gogh
was a great artist.

2 really good

This movie is great!

Fantastic!

Brilliant!

ground

what you walk
on outside

Kevin's ice
cream fell on
the ground.

group

a number of people
or things together

a group of runners

grow (grew, grown)

get bigger

My sunflower
grew quickly.

grown-up

an adult

Aunt Izzie is a grown-up.
Maisie is a child.

guess

try to give an answer
to something that you
do not know

Can you guess how many
candies are in this jar?

guest

someone who comes
to visit or stay

Uncle Frank is
our guest.

guinea pig

a small, furry animal
that squeaks

Zara's pet guinea
pig is named Blob.

guitar

a musical instrument
with strings

an electric
guitar

a b c d e f **g** h i j k l m n o p q r s t u v w x y z

Hh

a
b
c
d
e
f
g
h
i
j
k
l
m
n
o
p
q
r
s
t
u
v
w
x
y
z

hair

Hair grows on your head and on some animals' bodies.

curly hair   straight hair

hairbrush

something you can use to make hair neat and get rid of knots and tangles

half (halves)

one of two parts of something that are both the same size

half a pizza

hammer

a tool you use to knock nails into something

hamster

a small, furry animal that people often keep as a pet

hand

the part of your body at the end of your arm

handle

something you hold onto or use to open or move something

a door handle

hang (hung, hung)

fix something so that it stays off the ground

Jen has hung her coat on a hook.

happen

take place

What will happen if Nico moves the red block?

happy

If you are happy, you are pleased about something and life feels good.

Pia is feeling happy.

hard

1 solid and not soft

a hard chair

2 difficult or not easy

$$23 \times 14 - 6 =$$

This is quite hard.

hashtag

The name for the sign # that people use in social media to show what a tweet or post is about.

hat

something you can wear on your head

different kinds of hats

hate

not like something or someone at all

Ben hates loud music.

have (had, had)

1 If you have something, it is yours.

Mimi has a lot of shoes.

2 feel or suffer something

Mingmei has a headache.

head

the part of your body that is on top of your neck

healthy

1 If you are healthy, you are not sick.

Dash is a very healthy cat.

2 Good food, fresh air and exercise are all healthy things.

hear (heard, heard)

notice sounds around you with your ears

a b c d e f g h i j k l m n o p q r s t u v w x y z

a b c d e f g **h** i j k l m n o p q r s t u v w x y z

heart

1 a special pump inside you that pushes blood around your body

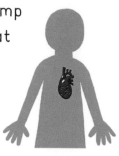

2 this shape, which makes people think about love

heat

make something warm or hot

Keith is heating some soup.

heavy

hard to lift or move

This box is very heavy.

HEAVY ⚠

height

how tall someone or something is

Jade is measuring the height of the table.

helicopter

a flying machine with blades that spin around very fast

hello

a word you say when you meet someone or answer the phone

Hello Manuel!   Hi Lucia!

helmet

a hard hat that keeps your head safe if you fall

help

do something to make things easier for someone

Faroz is helping Bea to put her shoes on.

hen

(also called a chicken) a bird that farmers keep for eggs and meat

hen   chick

hide (hid, hidden)

1 go to a place where nobody can see you

George is hiding under the box.

44

2 put something where nobody can see it

This squirrel is hiding a nut.

high

a long way above the ground

a high building

highchair

a chair that babies or small children sit in for their meals

hill

a piece of land that is higher than the land around it

hippopotamus

(also called a hippo)

a very big animal with short legs and little ears

history

information about what happened in the past

I love books about history.

hit (hit, hit)

bang or knock something or someone hard

Zoe is going to hit the ball.

hold (held, held)

have something in your hands or your arms

Peter is holding a pen.

hole

a space or gap in something

There's a hole in my sock!

home

where you and your family live

a b c d e f g h i j k l m n o p q r s t u v w x y z

a
b
c
d
e
f
g
h
i
j
k
l
m
n
o
p
q
r
s
t
u
v
w
x
y
z

honey

sweet, sticky liquid that bees make and people eat

hop

jump on one leg

Isaac is hopping.

horse

a big animal with four legs and a long tail. People ride horses.

hot

very warm

I'm so hot!

hotel

a building with lots of bedrooms that people pay to stay in

hour

a part of each day that lasts 60 minutes

There are 24 hours in a day.

The small hand shows the hours.

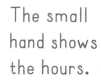

house

a building that people live in

hug

wrap your arms around someone and hold them tightly

I like hugging Gran!

hungry

If you are hungry, you feel you need to eat something.

This dog is hungry.

hurry

go fast

Xanthe is hurrying to get to school.

hurt (hurt, hurt)

If something hurts, you feel pain.

Germaine's arm really hurts.

Ii

ice
hard, frozen water

a block of ice

ice cream
a very cold, sweet food made from milk or cream

icon
a small picture on a phone or computer that opens an app

idea
something new that pops into your head

I have a great idea!

insect
a small animal with six legs

Bumblebees are insects.

inside
1 in something

There is a lizard inside this tank.

2 in a building and not outside

Lara has to stay inside today.

instead
in place of something

Tia chose pasta instead of pizza.

instrument
something you play to make music

A triangle is a musical instrument.

internet
the way that computers all over the world share information

invite
ask someone to come somewhere or do something

I've invited ten people to my party.

iron
a machine that makes clothes smooth when it gets hot

island
a piece of land with water all around it

itch
If your skin itches, you want to scratch it.

Ben's chin is itching.

a b c d e f g h i j k l m n o p q r s t u v w x y z

47

Jj

a b c d e f g h i j k l m n o p q r s t u v w x

jacket

a short coat that covers the top of your body

a green jacket

jar

a container for keeping things in. Jars are usually made of glass.

jeans

pants made from a strong material called denim

a pair of jeans

jigsaw

a picture cut into pieces that people enjoy putting back together again

job

1 what someone does to earn money

These are two different jobs.

scientist   plumber

2 something that needs doing

Painting this room is a big job.

join

1 become part of a club or group

Olly has joined the basketball team.

2 fix two things together

Sophie is joining two pieces of wood together.

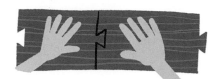

joke

something someone says that makes people laugh

What's the fastest vegetable?

A runner bean!

journey

a trip from one place to another

Owen and Jon are starting a journey.

juggle

keep two or more things in the air at the same time by throwing and catching them one after the other

juice
liquid from fruit and vegetables when they are squeezed or squashed

orange juice

jump
push yourself into the air using your legs

Mahir is jumping.

jungle
a thick, steamy forest in a hot country

Kk

kangaroo
an Australian animal that moves by jumping, using its big back legs

keep (kept, kept)
have something and not give it away

I want to keep all my baby toys.

key
something you use to open, lock or unlock a door

keyboard
1 the part of a computer with letters and numbers on it

2 a musical instrument such as an electric piano

kick
hit something using your foot

Paolo has kicked the ball.

kid
1 a word people use for "child"

Lauryn is such a friendly kid.

2 a baby goat

kill
make something die

Paolo's ball has killed Aunt Em's plant.

a b c d e f g h i j **k** l m n o p q r s t u v w x y z

a b c d e f g h i j **k** l m n o p q r s t u v w x y z

kind¹

If you are kind, you care about people and help them.

Nisha is very kind.

kind²

a type or sort of something

Here are some different kinds of shoes.

king

a man who rules a country because his family did before him

kiss

touch someone or something gently with your lips

Nia is kissing her doll.

kitchen

a place where people prepare and cook food

kite

a toy that flies around in the sky if the wind is blowing

kitten

a young cat

a sweet little kitten

knee

the bony part in the middle of your leg where it bends

kneel

(knelt, knelt)

get down onto your knees

Yasmin is kneeling.

knife (knives)

something with a handle and a sharp edge that you use to cut things

knight

a soldier who lived a long time ago

knock

hit something

Jay is knocking on the door.

knot

where something such as string or rope is tied

know (knew, known)

1 If you know someone, you have met before.

Adil knows Jake from school.

2 have some information, or a skill, in your mind

I'm so glad I know how to read.

Ll

ladder
something you climb to reach high places

a long ladder

lady (ladies)
a woman

two ladies smiling

ladybug
a small, red or yellow beetle with black spots

lake
a large area of water surrounded by land

lamb
a young sheep

lamp
something you switch on that gives out light

land
parts of the Earth that are not covered in water

The land is green in this picture.

language
the words people use to speak and write

What language do you speak?

Ich spreche Deutsch.*

large
big; taking up a lot of space

a very large dog

last
1 If you are last, you are at the end of something.

The red car is last.

2 the time before this

Alesha planted this tree last year.

late
1 after the right time

09:45 - EXPECTED 10:05

The train is late.

*I speak German.

a
b
c
d
e
f
g
h
i
j
k
l
m
n
o
p
q
r
s
t
u
v
w
x
y
z

2 near the end of something

Geoff watches TV until late at night.

laugh
make sounds that show you think something is funny

Sunil is laughing.

lead¹ (led, led)
go first to show someone the way

Emma is leading.

lead² (led, led)
be connected to something

What does this wire lead to?

leaf (leaves)
one of the thin, flat parts of a plant or tree

a maple leaf

lean
bend over to one side

The Leaning Tower of Pisa

learn
get to know and understand something new

Ava is learning to ride a bike.

leave (left, left)
1 go away from somewhere

The band has left the stage.

2 let something stay where it is

Someone has left a hat on this bench.

left
the side opposite to the right side

Joshua writes with his left hand.

leg
the long part of your body between your bottom and foot

lemon
a yellow fruit that tastes sour

length
how long something is

The length of this box is 8 inches.

less

not as much as

Ian has less hair than Freddie.

lesson

a time when someone teaches you something

a singing lesson

let (let, let)

allow something to happen

Alice let her balloon fly away.

letter

1 a message you write on paper

Dear Aunt Rani,

Thank you for the socks. I always need more.

Love from Greta

2 a sign or symbol you use to write words with

A, B and C are all letters.

A B C

lettuce

a green, leafy vegetable that you eat in a salad

library (libraries)

somewhere that lets you take books home to read

Libraries have thousands of books.

lid

a top that covers something, such as a jar or box

lid

lie¹ (lay, lain)

rest with your body flat on something

Dot is lying on the mat.

lie²

say something that is not true

Have you seen my cake?

This boy is lying.

No...

life (lives)

the time when someone or something is alive

Aunt Flo loves life.

lift

pick something up

The crane is lifting the box.

a b c d e f g h i j k **l** m n o p q r s t u v w x y z

In English, some words have several very different meanings. The word "light" has four.

light[1]

1 You need light to see things. It comes from lamps and from the Sun.

2 another word for a lamp

Switch the light off, please.

light[2]

1 not weighing much; not heavy

A feather is very light.

2 If a color is light, it is pale and not dark.

a light orange scarf

like[1]

If you like someone or something, you think they are good or nice.

Mrs. Patterson likes soccer.

like[2]

similar in some way

Nellie looks like her sister Ellie.

line

1 a long, thin mark like this

2 a group of people or things in a row

a line of trees

lion

a big, wild animal with sharp teeth and claws

lip

one of the two outside parts of your mouth

liquid

something you can pour, that is not solid or hard

list

something you write to help you remember what to buy or do

☐ tidy my room
☐ read my book
☐ call Gran

listen

make sure you hear and understand something

Pedro is listening to a podcast.

little

small; not big

a little bird

live

1 If you live in a place, it is your home.

Fish live in water.

2 Someone or something that lives is alive.

Tortoises live for a long time.

lock

something that keeps doors and boxes shut

log

a piece of wood that has been cut from a tree

long

If something is long, one end is far from the other end.

Natalie has very long hair.

look

1 use your eyes to see something

Dave is looking up.

2 seem to be or appear

This plant looks very healthy.

lose (lost, lost)

1 not be able to find something

Mr. Baker has lost his glasses.

2 If you lose a game or match, you do not win it.

The Larks lost the match.

| 3 | LARKS vs. JAYS | 5 |

lot

a large number or amount

a lot of pens

loud

making a lot of noise

Those drums are very loud.

love

like someone or something very much

Liv loves her pet rabbit.

low

near the ground

a low table

lunch

a meal you eat in the middle of the day

a healthy lunch

a b c d e f g h i j k l m n o p q r s t u v w x y z

a b c d e f g h i j k l **m** n o p q r s t u v w x y z

Mm

machine

something with moving parts that work together to do a job

an ice cream machine

magic

In stories, magic is the power that makes incredible things happen.

I blame magic.

mail

emails in your inbox

NEW MAIL

main

the most important or the biggest

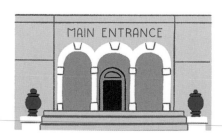
MAIN ENTRANCE

make (made, made)

1 put the pieces of something together

I made this blanket.

2 If you make something happen, it happens because of what you do.

Mr. Evans made the choir practice.

man (men)

a boy who has grown up

man

boy

mango

a big, juicy fruit with a flat pit in the middle

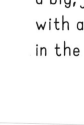

many (more, most)

a large number; a lot of

There are many different kinds of butterflies.

map

a picture that shows where places are

market

a place where you can buy different things

Many markets are outdoors.

mask

something people wear to cover their faces

a tiger mask

match[1]

1 a game that two teams, pairs or people play against each other

a tennis match

2 a small stick that makes fire when you rub its tip against the box it comes in

match[2]

If things match, they are the same in some way.

This coat matches these boots

matter

1 If something matters, it is important.

It doesn't matter which way I go.

2 If something is the matter, there is a problem.

What's the matter with Steve's bike?

meal

food you eat at special times of the day

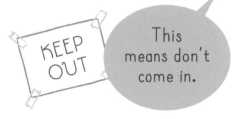

a healthy meal

mean (meant, meant)

If you say what something means, you explain it.

KEEP OUT

This means don't come in.

measure

find out how tall, long, big or heavy something is

Levi is measuring how tall he is.

meat

a kind of food that comes from animals

a piece of meat

media

all the ways people get news, information or stories through phones, tablets, newspapers, televisions and so on

medicine

something you take to make you feel better when you are sick

meet (met, met)

If you meet someone, you both go to the same place at the same time.

Robin and Eliot always meet at the bus stop.

a b c d e f g h i j k l m n o p q r s t u v w x y z

a
b
c
d
e
f
g
h
i
j
k
l
m
n
o
p
q
r
s
t
u
v
w
x
y
z

mend

fix something that is broken

Dad is mending Lou's toy.

mess

something that is untidy and sometimes dirty

What a mess!

message

words you write or send to someone when you cannnot speak to them

Meet you at 3pm.

a text message

metal

hard stuff that comes out of the ground. Gold and silver are metals.

a metal spoon

microwave

a little oven that cooks or heats food very quickly

PING!

middle

the place that is the same distance from all the sides or ends of something

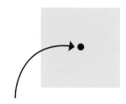

the middle of the square

milk

white liquid you can drink. There are several kinds of milk.

mind

the part of you that thinks, remembers and imagines things

My mind is always full of ideas.

minus

the word you use when you take away one number from another

$$3 - 1 = 2$$

the minus sign

minute

60 seconds of time. There are 60 minutes in an hour.

It is 5 minutes past 6.

mirror

a special piece of glass that you can see yourself in

miss

1 feel sad because someone is not with you

I miss my friends.

2 be too late for

Harry missed the bus.

mistake

If you make a mistake, you do something wrong.

Can you spot the spelling mistake?

verb
mishtake
writing

mix

add things together to make one thing

You can mix red and blue paint to make purple.

model

a small copy of something

a model rocket

money

coins and bills that you use to buy things

monkey

an animal with a long tail and long arms and legs

month

a part of a year that lasts about four weeks. There are 12 months in each year.

moon

a huge, bright ball of rock that you can often see in the sky at night

more

a bigger amount

Belle has more hair than Tyson.

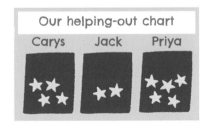

morning

the first part of the day, before noon at 12 o'clock.

I eat breakfast in the morning.

most

the biggest amount

Our helping-out chart		
Carys	Jack	Priya

Who has the most stars?

moth

an insect with a hairy body and four wings

a
b
c
d
e
f

l
m
n
o
p
q
r
s
t
u
v
w
x
y
z

motorcycle
a big, heavy bicycle with an engine

mountain
a very high piece of land

These mountains are covered with snow.

mouse (mice)
1 a small, furry animal with a long tail

2 something you use to move around on a computer screen

mouth
the part of your face that you use for speaking and eating

move
1 go from one place to another

Sam is moving from the sun into the shade.

2 go to live somewhere different

The Barker family is moving to the country.

3 take something from one place to another

The ants are moving leaves along the branch.

much (more, most)
a large amount

That's too much pasta for me!

mud
sticky, wet dirt

This dog is covered in mud!

museum
somewhere you go to see old or interesting things

a dinosaur skeleton in a museum

mushroom
a kind of fungus, often shaped like a little umbrella

music
sounds you make when you sing or play a musical instrument

Charlie loves music.

Nn

nail

1 one of the hard parts at the ends of your fingers and toes

2 a pointed metal thing that you use to join pieces of wood together

name

what you call someone or something

My pet's name is Shelly.

narrow

If something is narrow, it is thin and not wide.

The gate is too narrow.

nature

everything in the world around us that is not made by people

naughty

If you are naughty, you do things you are not supposed to do

a naughty seagull

near

not far away from; close to

The cup is near the edge.

neck

the part of your body that joins your head to the rest of your body

necklace

a pretty thing you can hang around your neck

a gold necklace

need

If you need something, you have to have it.

I need a haircut!

needle

1 a thin, sharp piece of metal that you use for sewing

2 a very thin piece of metal used for putting medicine into someone's body

needle

a b c d e f g h i j k l m **n** o p q r s t u v w x y z

a b c d e f g h i j k l m n o p q r s t u v w x y z

neighbor

someone who lives near you

We are neighbors.

nest

the home that birds and some animals make for their eggs and babies

net

1 something you use to catch fish and other animals

2 something you hit the ball over or into in some games

a badminton net

nervous

If you are nervous about something, you are worried about it.

Deon is nervous about a test at school.

never

at no time; not ever

This t-shirt will never fit me again.

new

1 not done, made or used before

This is Derek's new car.

2 different from how things were before

Mr. Patel is our new math teacher.

Welcome, Mr. Patel

news

information about things that are happening in the world, or to you

I passed my exam!

Joe has some good news.

newspaper

some sheets of paper with stories and photographs about the news

next

1 the one after this one

We're going to the zoo next Wednesday.

2 nearest to

The motorcycle is next to the van.

nice

If you think something is nice, you like it.

Mmm, this ice cream is nice.

night

the time when it is dark outside and people sleep

nod

move your head up and down. If you nod, it often means "yes."

Anna is nodding.

noise

sounds that someone or something makes

Dee's trumpet makes a lot of noise.

noisy

making a lot of loud sounds

Helicopters are very noisy.

PARDON?

nose

the part of your body that you use to smell and breathe

note

1 one sound you make when you sing or play some music

2 a short message

Back in 5 minutes

notebook

a book with empty pages for you to write on

notice

see and know about

Callum has noticed that his shoe is untied.

now

at this time

We're leaving now.

OK, see you soon!

number

a word or a symbol that tells you how many there are of something

the number 8

8

nurse

someone who looks after people who are sick

Ayaz is a nurse.

nut

a seed with a hard shell

You can eat this kind of nut.

a b c d e f g h i j k l m **n** o p q r s t u v w x y z

Oo

a b c d e f g h i j k l m n **o** p q r s t u v w x y z

ocean

a very large sea

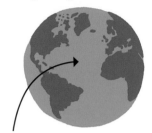

This ocean is called the Atlantic Ocean.

o'clock

a word you sometimes use when you say what time it is

It's 4 o'clock.

octopus

an animal that lives in the sea and has eight long arms

odd

1 If a number is odd, you cannot divide it by two.

①2③4⑤

Here, all the odd numbers have a circle around them.

2 a bit unusual

Hans has an odd mustache.

offer¹

say you will do something for someone

Mari is offering to carry Nia's bags.

offer²

a cheaper price than usual

SPECIAL OFFER

Half price

office

a room or building where people work. Most have desks and computers.

often

regularly or a lot of times

Squirrels often eat nuts.

oil

a thick, sticky liquid. Some kinds of oil make engines or machines work. Other kinds you can cook with.

olive oil

old

1 Someone who is old has lived for a very long time.

Mr. Javid is very old. He's 94.

64

2 not new; made or bought some time ago

an old car

once
one time only

Tim only went skiing once.

onion
a round vegetable with thin skin and a very strong smell and flavor

online
on the internet

Bonnie is checking something online.

only
just; no more than

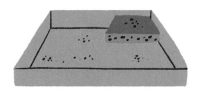

There's only one left.

open[1]
1 move a door, gate or window so something can go through it

2 unwrap, or take the lid or top off something

Lulu opened her present.

open[2]
If something is open, you can go through it or into it.

an open gate

opposite[1]
the thing that is the most different than another thing

"Small" is the opposite of "big."

I knew that!

Can you think of the opposites of these words?

happy   quiet   good

opposite[2]
facing each other

These frogs are sitting opposite each other.

orange
1 a round, juicy fruit with thick skin

2 a color

a b c d e f g h i j k l m n o p q r s t u v w x y z

a b c d e f g h i j k l m n **o** p q r s t u v w x y z

order[1]

1 ask for something in a café or restaurant

I'm going to order lasagne.

2 pay for something to be delivered

Zelda has ordered a new watch.

3 tell someone that they must do something

Greg ordered his dog to sit.

Sit!

other

1 different

Can I try some other glasses please?

2 one of two

Where is the other glove?

outside

1 in the open air, not inside a building

Wild birds live outside.

2 not in something, but near it

Bob left his bag outside the tent.

over

1 on top of

Fatima wears a hijab over her hair.

2 finished

The movie is over.

THE END

3 down

Theo fell over.

4 above or across

The hot-air balloon floated over our house.

owl

a bird that flies at night

own

If you own something, it is yours.

Zach owns five pairs of sneakers.

Pp

page
a sheet of paper in a book

the first page

paint[1]
a thick liquid you use to add color to things

containers of paint

paint[2]
1 make a picture with paints and a paintbrush

2 change the color of something

Ivy is painting her toenails blue.

pair
If two things are a pair, they go together.

a pair of slippers

pale
If a color is pale, it is light and not dark.

pale green

pale blue

panda
a big black and white bear that lives in China

paper
a sheet you write or draw on, or wrap things up in

wrapping paper

parachute
a big piece of cloth that carries someone safely from a plane to the ground

parent
a mother or father

These are my parents.

park[1]
an open space where people can relax, walk or play

park[2]
leave a car somewhere

Dad found a space to park.

a b c d e f g h i j k l m n o **p** q r s t u v w x y z

67

a
b
c
d
e
f
g
h
i
j
k
l
m
n
o
p
q
r
s
t
u
v
w
x
y
z

parrot

a colorful bird that people sometimes keep as a pet

part

a piece of something bigger

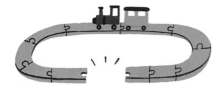

Part of the track is missing.

partner

someone you do something with

tennis partners

party

when friends meet to eat, drink and have fun together

a costume party

pass

1 go past someone or something

The boat is passing the castle.

2 hand something to someone

Pass the ketchup, please!

3 do well on a test

Ali passed the spelling test.

past¹

the time before now

In the past, some people traveled by coach.

past²

by or beside

The bus goes past the school.

path

a narrow road or track for people to walk on

paw

an animal's foot

a cat's paw

pay (paid, paid)

give someone money for something

Jenny is paying for an ice cream.

pea

a small, green, round vegetable that grows in a pod

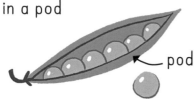

pod

peach

a soft, juicy fruit with furry skin and a pit in the middle

peak

the very top of a mountain

a snowy peak

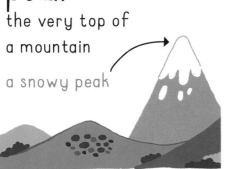

peanut

a small, oval nut that people often roast and eat

pear

a sweet, juicy fruit with a yellow or green skin

pebble

a smooth, round stone that you find on beaches

pen

something you write with

a fountain pen

pencil

a thin, wooden stick with a black middle that you can write or draw with

penguin

a black and white bird that cannot fly

Penguins are great swimmers.

people

men, women and children

There are four people here.

pepper

1 grains or powder that you sprinkle on food to add flavor

2 a vegetable that can be red, orange, yellow or green

pepperoni

spicy meat that people often put on top of pizzas

person

a man, woman or child

This person has black hair.

pet

an animal that you keep in your home

This hamster is Erin's pet.

a b c d e f g h i j k l m n o **p** q r s t u v w x y z

a b c d e f g h i j k l m n o **p** q r s t u v w x y z

phone
(short for "telephone")

something you use to speak to someone who is not with you

a cell phone

photograph

a picture taken with a camera or cell phone

a vacation photograph

piano

a musical instrument with black and white keys that you play with your fingers

pick

1 choose

Tim picked the fluffy rabbit.

2 take fruit or flowers from a bush, tree or plant

Louisa picked a strawberry.

picnic

a meal you eat outdoors

picture

a photograph, painting or drawing

a picture of a city

piece

one part of something

a piece of cake

pillow

something soft you rest your head on when you sleep

pilot

someone who flies planes

pineapple

a large fruit with prickly skin and hard, pointed leaves

pizza

a flat bread base cooked with other food on top

place

somewhere; a particular spot. A place can be very big, like a city, or small, like a garden.

I love this place.

plan¹
a map of a building
or a place

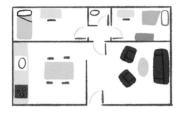

a house plan

plan²
think about something
and then decide
how to do it

Adie is planning
what to cook.

plane
(short for airplane)
a big machine that flies
in the sky

planet
an enormous, ball-shaped
thing that moves around
the Sun in space

Saturn is a planet.

plant¹
a living thing that grows
in soil or water

Trees and
flowers
are plants.

plant²
put seeds or plants in the
ground so they can grow

Finn is planting
flowers.

plate
a round, flat dish that
you put food on

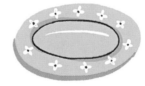

play
1 do something just
for fun

Leila is playing with
her friends.

2 If you can
play a musical
instrument,
you can make
music with it.

Tess is playing
the saxophone.

3 take part in a sport
or game

Cleo and Dev are
playing a game.

playground
an outdoor space where
children can play

please
a word you should
always say when you
ask for something

Can I have a
drink please?

a b c d e f g h i j k l m n o p q r s t u v w x y z

a b c d e f g h i j k l m n o p q r s t u v w x y z

plum

a small, soft, juicy fruit with red, yellow or purple skin.

pocket

a small bag that is a part of your clothes. You can keep things in a pocket.

Luke's shirt has two pockets.

podcast

a radio program you can download and listen to when you want to

poem

a piece of writing that may have short lines and words that rhyme

My dog

My dog is my best friend, and I know that I am hers.
When we go to the beach together
She digs big holes in the sand.

point¹

1 the sharp end of something

This pencil has a sharp point.

2 part of the score in a game

| 5 | Reds | Blues | 3 |

The Reds have five points.

point²

use your finger to show where something is

Laura is pointing at a butterfly.

police

people whose job is to stop people from breaking the law

pollution

something bad that spoils the environment, such as waste or fumes

pond

a small area of water, often in a garden

pony (ponies)

a small horse that children often ride

pool

a place where people go to swim or play in water

poor

1 a word you might use to describe someone who has not got enough money

In stories, the hero is often poor.

2 a word you use when you feel sorry for someone

Poor Megan!

post

a message, video or some writing someone puts on a social media site

potato (potatoes)

a vegetable that grows under the ground. You can cook potatoes in lots of different ways.

present

something you give to someone or that they give to you to be kind

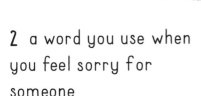

press

push on something

PRESS THE RED BUTTON

pretend

act as if something is true when it is not

Lem is pretending to fly.

pretty

nice to look at

a pretty flowerpot

price

how much something costs

2 for the price of 1

prince

the son of a king or queen or the husband of a princess

princess

the daughter of a king or queen or the wife of a prince

prize

something you can win in a competition

1st

Pickle won first prize.

a b c d e f g h i j k l m n o **p** q r s t u v w x y z

a
b
c
d
e
f
g
h
i
j
k
l
m
n
o
p
q
r
s
t
u
v
w
x
y
z

promise
say you really will
do something

I promise
I won't drop
you!

puddle
a small pool of water
on the ground

Puddles often
appear after
rain.

pull
move someone or
something towards you

The girls pulled on
the rope.

pumpkin
a very large, round fruit
with a hard orange or
yellow skin

punctuation
the marks you add to
a piece of writing that
make it easier to read
and understand

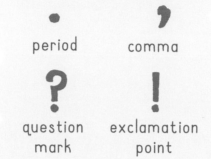

Here are some kinds
of punctuation:

.
period

,
comma

?
question
mark

!
exclamation
point

puppet
a kind of doll that
you can make move

a glove
puppet

puppy (puppies)
a young dog

push
move someone or
something away from you

Max is pushing
the cart.

put (put, put)
move something
to a place

Edie put a
cherry on
top of
her cake.

puzzle
a game you need to
think about carefully

a word puzzle

Qq

quarter

one of four pieces of something that are all the same size

a quarter

queen

a woman who rules a country because her family did before her

Cleopatra was a very famous queen.

question

something you say or write when you want an answer

question   answer

quick

1 moving fast; speedy

Anthony's boat is very quick.

2 not lasting long

The wheelchair race was so quick!

quiet

not making much noise

The princess had to be very quiet.

quite

1 a bit; fairly; rather

Horses are quite big, but elephants are bigger.

2 completely

Jade hasn't quite finished her painting.

quiz

a game in which you have to answer questions

Who will win the quiz?

a b c d e f g h i j k l m n o p **q** r s t u v w x y z

75

Rr

rabbit
a small, furry animal with long ears and a fluffy tail

race
a competition to see who is the fastest

radio
a machine that plays music or things you can listen to

rain
When it rains, little drops of water fall from the sky.

rainbow
a curve of different colors that can appear in the sky if the sun shines when it is raining

raspberry
(raspberries)
a small, soft, dark pink fruit

rat
a small animal with sharp teeth and a long tail

reach
1 be able to get to or touch

I can't reach it.

2 arrive somewhere

Kitty has reached the other side of the pool.

read (read, read)
look at letters and words and be able to understand them

ready
able to do something immediately

Lola is ready to start the running race.

real
1 not a copy; not fake

This necklace is real gold.

2 true and not made up

REAL LIFE STORIES!

recipe

a list of things you need and what to do to make something to eat or drink

a recipe book

recorder

a musical instrument that you blow into to make sounds

recycle

to use something again, or make it into something new

I recycle everything I can.

refrigerator

(also called a fridge)

a metal cabinet that keeps food cold

remember

think of something that happened or something you learned in the past

Alf remembers riding his first motorcycle.

reply (replied, replied)

answer a question or a message

Are you going to the party?

Yes I am.

Ravi is replying to Aunt Fi's question.

rescue

save someone or something from danger

Erik will soon rescue the cat.

rhinoceros

(also called a rhino)

a large animal with thick skin and horns on its nose

ribbon

a long, thin strip of cloth that you can use to decorate gifts or tie up your hair

rice

seeds from a kind of grass plant that you can cook and eat

rich

If you are rich, you have plenty of money.

Martha is rich.

a b c d e f g h i j k l m n o p q **r** s t u v w x y z

ride (rode, ridden)

sit on something and move forwards

Seb is trying to ride a donkey.

right

1 without any mistakes

Rose got all the answers right.

2 the side opposite to the left side

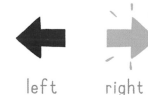

left right

ring¹

something pretty that you wear on your finger

ring² (rang, rung)

When a phone or bell rings, it makes a sound.

ripe

If fruit is ripe, it is soft and ready to eat.

Bananas turn yellow when they are ripe.

river

a wide strip of water that flows across land to the sea

road

a hard strip of ground that goes from one place to another

robot

a machine built to do some of the things people do

a robot in a factory

rock

a very big stone

rocket

a machine that can take astronauts up into space

roof

the top part of a building

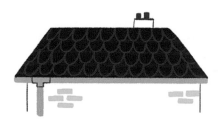

room

an area inside a building that has walls around it and a door to get into it

Jem's room is very messy.

78

rope

something made of lots of threads twisted together to make one strong one

rose

a flower with a thorny stem

round

shaped like a circle or a bubble

a round window

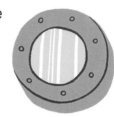

rug

something that covers only part of a floor

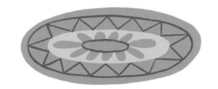

ruler

a flat strip for measuring things and drawing straight lines

rush

go quickly; hurry

It started to rain, so we rushed inside.

Ss

sad

not feeling happy

Leon is sad.

safe

1 not in any danger

We're safe in here.

2 If something is safe, it is not dangerous.

a safe place to cross

sailor

someone who works on a ship

salad

a mixture of raw vegetables, beans or other cold food

salt

white powder that you put on food or use in cooking to add flavor

a b c d e f g h i j k l m n o p q r s t u v w x y z

a b c d e f g h i j k l m n o p q r **s** t u v w x y z

same
Things that are the same are just like each other.

the same t-shirt

sand
a mixture of tiny bits of rock and shell. You find sand on some beaches and in deserts.

sandal
a kind of shoe that you wear when it is hot

sandwich
two pieces of bread with other kinds of food between them

sausage
chopped-up food inside a special skin

save
1 rescue someone from danger

Edward saved the teddy bear from the water.

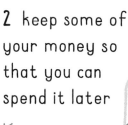

2 keep some of your money so that you can spend it later

Kian saves coins in a jar.

3 click on something to keep your work safe on a computer

I always save my work.

saw
a tool for cutting wood

say (said, said)
speak some words

I'm up here!

What did you say?

scared
afraid or frightened

Jaden is scared of wasps.

scarf (scarves)
a long, thin piece of clothing that keeps your neck warm

school
a place where children go to learn

scissors

something you use to cut things with

a pair of scissors

scooter

something with two wheels that you ride on

screen

the flat part of a phone or computer that you look at

sea

an enormous area of salty water

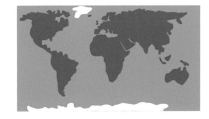

The sea is blue on this map.

seal

an animal that lives in the sea and on land.

search

look for very hard

Mel and Thomas are searching for Tilly.

seat

a chair or bench that you sit on

theater seats

secret

something you do not want everyone to know

Non is telling Will a secret.

see (saw, seen)

1 use your eyes to notice something

I can see a tiny bird!

2 meet up with someone

See you next week!

sell (sold, sold)

let someone have something if they give you money

Eve is selling apples.

send (sent, sent)

make someone or something go somewhere

Balik is sending a package.

a b c d e f g h i j k l m n o p q r s t u v w x y z

sentence

a group of words that begins with a capital letter, ends with a period and makes sense

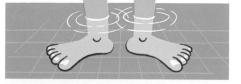

I like swimming in the sea.

a sentence

sew (sewed, sewn)

join pieces of cloth together with a needle and some thread

shadow

a dark shape that appears when something blocks the light

Tigger's shadow

shake (shook, shaken)

move something quickly up and down or from side to side

shallow

not very deep

This pool is shallow.

shampoo

a kind of soap you use when you wash your hair

share

let someone have a part of something or use something with you

Manu is sharing his pencils with Amy.

shark

a large fish with sharp teeth

sharp

If something is sharp, it has a very thin edge or a pointed end that can cut or prick you.

a very sharp thorn

sheep (sheep)

an animal with a thick, woolly coat

sheet

1 a flat piece of paper, glass or plastic

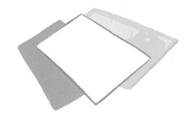

2 a piece of cloth you put on a bed to lie on

sheet

a b c d e f g h i j k l m n o p q r s t u v w x y z

shelf (shelves)

a flat piece of metal, wood or plastic that is fixed to a wall

shell

the hard cover around something

shell

ship

a very big boat that carries people and things over the sea

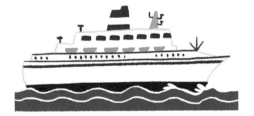

shirt

something you wear on the top half of your body

Many shirts have buttons and a collar.

shoe

something you wear to cover your foot

a pair of shoes

shop

buy things in a store or online

short

1 not very long

This dog has a short, curly tail.

2 not very tall

tall

short

shorts

pants with short legs

a pair of shorts

shoulder

one of the bony parts at the very top of your arm

shout

say something very loudly

Bez is shouting.

show¹
(showed, shown)

1 let someone see something

Lesley is showing her friend her drawings.

2 explain how to do something by doing it yourself

Priti showed me how to dance bhangra.

show²

a program on television, or something you see at a theater

a b c d e f g h i j k l m n o p q r s t u v w x y z

83

a b c d e f g h i j k l m n o p q r s t u v w x y z

shower

1 something that sends drops of water over your body to wash it

2 rain that only falls for a short time

I'm sure it's only a shower.

shrink (shrank, shrunk)

become or make smaller

Bella's sock has shrunk.

shut (shut, shut)

move a door or a cover to block a space; close

Wilf is shutting the door.

side

1 the edge of something

a square has four equal sides

2 the flat surface of something

A sheet of paper has two sides.

3 a team

The Blues are the winning side.

sign¹

1 words or pictures that tell you what to do

SLOW DOWN

2 a shape that means something

@ is the sign for "at."

sign²

1 write your name

This is how James signs his name.

2 communicate using the language that people who cannot hear well may use

Ethan is signing "Hello" in one kind of sign language.

silence

when there is no sound at all

Silence please!

since

from this time

We have been standing in this line since noon.

SHOW TONIGHT!

sing (sang, sung)
make music with
your voice

sink¹
something you
wash things
in, such as
your hands
and face

sink² (sank, sunk)
go downwards, often
in water

My boat
sank!

sit (sat, sat)
rest your bottom
on something

Joseph is
sitting on
the floor.

size
how big or small
something is

I think these
shoes are the
wrong size.

skate
move along wearing
special boots called skates

Lena is
skating on
the ice.

skateboard
a flat board with wheels
that you can ride and do
tricks on

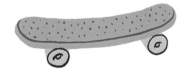

skeleton
All the bones in a body
make a skeleton.

a fish skeleton

ski
glide along
on snow wearing
two long, flat things
called skis on your feet

ski

skin
1 the outside cover
of your body

2 the layer that covers
a fruit or vegetable

Oranges have a
very thick skin.

skirt
a piece of clothing
that hangs down from
the waist

a b c d e f g h i j k l m n o p q r s t u v w x y z

85

a b c d e f g h i j k l m n o p q r s t u v w x y z

sky (skies)

the space above the ground where you can see the sun, clouds, stars, planes and birds

sleep (slept, slept)

close your eyes and let your whole body rest

Tamara is sleeping.

sleeve

the part of your clothes that covers some or all of your arm

slice

a piece of something cut from something bigger

a slice of bread

slide¹

something you can play on in playgrounds

slide² (slid, slid)

move smoothly over or down something else

Peter is sliding down the hill.

slip

fall over by mistake

Fred slipped on the ice.

slipper

a soft, comfortable shoe that you wear indoors

slow

not very fast; taking a long time to do something or go somewhere

Tortoises are very slow.

slug

a soft animal without legs, like a snail without a shell

small

little; not big or tall

Ants are small.

smartphone

a cell phone that has apps and connects to the internet

smell

1 find out about something using your nose

Kit is smelling a flower.

86

2 If something smells, you notice it with your nose.

These boots smell bad!

smile
turn both corners of your mouth up because you are happy, or think something is funny

smoke
a gray or white cloud that comes from something that is burning

smooth
without any lumps or bumps on it

Apples have a smooth skin.

snail
a small, soft animal that lives in a shell it carries on its back

snake
a long, thin animal with no arms or legs

sneeze
a loud noise you make when air rushes out of your nose and mouth very fast

achoo!

snow
small, white pieces of ice that fall from the sky when it is very cold

soap
something you use to wash yourself

social media
websites and apps that help you talk to other people and share pictures, ideas and thoughts

sock
something you wear on your foot inside your shoe

sofa
a long, soft chair for two or more people

soft
not hard or firm

Ooh, this is so soft!

a b c d e f g h i j k l m n o p q r s t u v w x y z

a b c d e f g h i j k l m n o p q r s t u v w x y z

song

music which has words that you can sing

Everyone loves this song.

soon

happening not long from now

Soon, Rosa's baby will be born.

sort¹

a type or kind

There are lots of different sorts of nuts. Here are just a few.

pistachio   walnut
almond

sort²

organize or arrange things

Richard has sorted his socks into pairs.

sound

something you hear

Bees make a buzzing sound.

soup

a liquid food. Soup can be made from many different things.

tomato soup

space

1 an empty place

There's a space for one more coat on the coat rack.

2 everything that is around the Earth, including stars and planets

spacecraft

a machine that travels in space

speak

(spoke, spoken) say some words

Mehmet is speaking into his phone.

special

1 better or more important than usual

Today is a special day. It's my birthday!

2 made to do a particular thing

Eddie has special gloves for gardening.

speed

how fast you are moving

spell[1]

write or say all the letters of a word in the right order

dictionary

This is how you spell "dictionary."

spell[2]

magic words used in stories that make amazing things happen

spend

(spent, spent)

1 use money to buy something

Andy is spending his money.

2 pass your time doing something

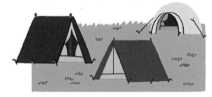

We spent last week camping in a field.

spider

a small animal with eight legs

spill

let some liquid fall out of something by mistake

Ibrahim has spilled some paint.

spinach

a vegetable with green leaves

splash

water flying up into the air

There was a splash in the lake.

sponge

something you can use to soak up liquid or to wash things

spoon

something you use for eating or to stir food

a wooden spoon

sport

a game with rules that you play to exercise and have fun

Basketball is a sport.

spot[1]

a small, round mark

This dog has lots of spots.

a b c d e f g h i j k l m n o p q r **s** t u v w x y z

a b c d e f g h i j k l m n o p q r s t u v w x y z

spot²

see or notice something

Can you spot the odd one out?

squirrel

a small animal with a furry tail

stairs

a set of steps inside a building that you walk up or down

stamp

a small piece of paper with a picture on it. You stick a stamp on a letter or package to show you have paid to mail it.

stand (stood, stood)

be on your feet, not sitting down

Wes is standing.

star

1 a small, bright light in the sky at night

2 a famous person

a movie star

start

do the first part of something; begin

Let's start!

station

a place that people go to get on or off a train

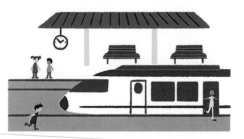

stay

1 not leave a place

We stayed in the park until the sun set.

2 live somewhere for a while

Matt stayed in a camper van for a week.

stick¹

a thin piece of wood

stick² (stuck, stuck)

fix something to another thing or use glue to fix things to each other

Marcus is sticking the shapes onto the paper.

still¹

not moving

The mouse stayed still when it heard the cat.

still²

not finished, stopped or gone

It's still snowing.

sting

(stung, stung)

If an animal or plant stings your skin, it hurts for a while.

A wasp stung Neil's arm.

stir

move something around with a spoon or stick

Alex is stirring the soup.

stone

a small piece of rock

stool

a chair without a back

stop

1 not move anymore

Cars must stop at the red light.

2 not happen anymore

Most birds stop singing at night.

storm

wild weather with rain, wind and sometimes thunder and lightning

story

words that tell you about something that has happened. Stories can be true or made up.

straight

without any bends or curves

a straight line

strawberry

(strawberries)

a soft, red fruit with tiny yellow seeds on the outside

a b c d e f g h i j k l m n o p q r s t u v w x y z

91

a b c d e f g h i j k l m n o p q r **s** t u v w x y z

street
a road in a town or city with houses, stores or other buildings

stress
a worried feeling you can get when you have a lot to do

Too much stress!

string
thin rope for tying things together

strong
1 able to lift heavy things

Sarah is very strong.

2 difficult to break

Steel is a very strong metal.

3 full of flavor

Garlic has a strong taste.

study
(studied, studied)
learn all about something

Romesh is studying hard.

suddenly
If something happens suddenly, it happens quickly and when you do not expect it.

Suddenly, the balloon popped.

sugar
sweet, white or brown grains or powder that you can add to food or drinks

sum
a math question that has numbers and the plus sign (+) in it

$$1 + 3 = 4$$

Sun
a very large, bright thing you may see in the sky in the day

sunflower
a very tall, yellow flower

sunglasses
glasses that protect your eyes from strong sunshine

supermarket
a big store that sells all sorts of different things

sure
If you are sure, you really believe something.

Leo is sure he will win.

surprise
something you do not expect to happen

What a lovely surprise!

swan
a big white or black bird with a long neck and large wings

sweep
(swept, swept)

use a brush to clean

Liam swept the floor.

sweet
1 lovely; cute

a sweet puppy

2 tasting like sugar

This cupcake tastes very sweet.

swim
(swam, swum)

move your body through water

swimming pool
a place filled with water for people to swim in

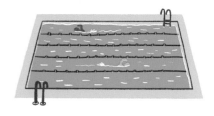

swimsuit
something you wear to go swimming

swing¹
something you sit on that goes backwards and forwards

swing²
(swung, swung)

move backwards and forwards

Kate is swinging in the hammock.

a b c d e f g h i j k l m n o p q r s t u v w x y z

Tt

a
b
c
d
e
f
g
h
i
j
k
l
m
n
o
p
q
r
s
t
u
v
w
x
y
z

table
a piece of furniture with legs and a flat top

tablet
1 a small, dry piece of medicine

2 a small computer you can carry around easily

tail
the part of some animals' bodies that grows out of their bottoms

take (took, taken)
1 move or carry something with you

I am taking my umbrella today.

2 steal something

Cara took a cupcake from the store.

$2.00

tale
a story

TALES OF ADVENTURE

talk
speak to someone

I feel a little sad.

Let's talk about it.

tall
If you are tall, your head is a long way from the ground.

taste
find out what food or drink is like by putting it into your mouth

This tastes delicious!

taxi
a car you pay to ride in

tea
a drink made by adding hot water to dried leaves

teacher

someone whose job is to teach people

Mrs. Lentern is our teacher.

team

a group of people who work or play a sport together

a soccer team

tear (tore, torn)

rip or damage something

Ned has torn his coat.

teddy bear

a furry toy that looks like a bear

telephone

(also called a phone)

something you use to speak to someone who is not with you

a cell phone

television

(also called a TV)

something that shows moving pictures and plays sounds

tell (told, told)

1 let someone know about something

Mark is telling a story.

text

2 say that someone must do something

Dad told Harvey to be quiet.

tent

a shelter made of strong cloth that you can sleep in outside

text

1 a message you send from one cell phone to another one

Almost here?

5 minutes!

2 writing in a book, newspaper or on a screen

There is a lot of text in this book.

a b c d e f g h i j k l m n o p q r s **t** u v w x y z

a b c d e f g h i j k l m n o p q r **s** t u v w x y z

thank

tell someone you are happy with something they have done for you or given you

Thank you for my present.

You're welcome!

theater

a building where people watch plays, shows and concerts on a stage

thin

1 narrow; not wide

a thin line

2 not weighing much; not fat

a thin dog

thing

something you see, do, touch or think about

a box full of different things

think
(thought, thought)

1 use your mind

Can you think of a place you like?

2 believe to be true

Jan thinks he is an astronaut.

thirsty

needing to drink something

Oh no! I'm so thirsty!

through

from one side to another

Elizabeth is coming through the gate.

throw
(threw, thrown)

make something move through the air

Helen has thrown the ball.

thumb

the shorter finger at the side of your hand

ticket

something that shows you have paid to do something or travel somewhere

tie
fix things together with a bow or knot using string, rope or ribbon

Oscar has tied his laces.

tiger
a big, wild animal with striped fur and sharp teeth

time
1 an exact moment
The time is 6 o'clock.

2 how long something takes to happen

Plants take time to grow.

tiny
very small indeed

a tiny bike

tip
the very end of something

the tip of Holly's finger

toast
a slice of bread that has been cooked until it is brown and crisp

toddler
a young child who is just starting to walk

toe
one of the five small parts at the end of your foot

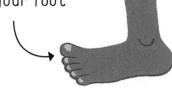

together
with another person or thing

Vera and Bruce eat together.

toilet
a special bowl with a seat that you sit on when you need to pee or poop

tomato
(tomatoes)
a soft, juicy fruit that you eat in salads or cook with

tongue
the long, soft part inside your mouth that you use to taste, eat and talk

Maryam is licking the ice cream with her tongue.

a b c d e f g h i j k l m n o p q r s **t** u v w x y z

tooth (teeth)

one of the hard, white things in your mouth that you use to bite and chew

a shark's tooth

toothbrush

a brush that you clean your teeth with

toothpaste

a thick liquid that you put on a toothbrush to clean your teeth

top

1 the highest part of something

There's a bird on the top of the shed.

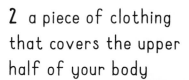

2 a piece of clothing that covers the upper half of your body

touch

put your hand or part of your body on or against something

Annie is touching the floor.

towel

a big, soft cloth that you use to dry your hands or your body

town

a place with stores, roads and houses where lots of people live and work

toy

something you can play with

This is Niall's best toy.

tractor

a big machine that farmers use to pull heavy things and do different jobs

traffic

everything traveling along a road

train

a big machine that moves on metal rails and carries a lot of people

trampoline

a metal frame covered with special cloth that you can bounce up and down on

tree

a very large plant with leaves, branches and a trunk

truck

a big machine that carries heavy loads from place to place

true

1 correct or right

A tomato is a fruit.

Yes, that's true.

2 If a story is true, it really happened.

AMAZING TRUE STORIES

try (tried, tried)

1 do your best to do something

Mina is trying to skate.

2 test something

Eliza is trying her soup.

t-shirt

a piece of clothing with short sleeves

turkey

a big bird that farmers keep for meat

turn¹

1 go in a different direction

TURN RIGHT HERE

2 move around

Oonagh is turning the key.

TV (also called a television)

something that shows moving pictures and plays sounds

twin

one of two children who have the same mother and were born at nearly the same time

type¹

a kind or sort of something

three types of fish

type²

use a keyboard to make words appear on a screen

My dinosaur project

99

a b c d e f g h i j k l m n o p q r s **t** u v w x y z

Uu

ugly
not very nice to look at

an ugly fish

umbrella
something you hold over your head to keep you dry when it rains

under
If something is under something else, it is lower than it.

Noah is under the slide.

understand
(understood, understood)
know what somebody means or how something works

Can you understand the instructions?

undress
take your clothes off

Oliver is undressing.

unfair
not right or kind

That's so unfair!

unhappy
sad or upset

Milo is unhappy.

uniform
clothes you wear to show you belong to a group

school uniform

universe
everything in space including the Earth, Sun, stars and planets

upset
not happy; sad

Jack is upset.

upside down
with the part usually at the top at the bottom

That painting is upside down!

use
do a job with something

I use a shovel to dig my garden.

useful
If something is useful, it helps you to do something more easily.

Bags are useful for carrying groceries.

usually
happening nearly every time

I usually tie my hair up for ballet.

Vv

vaccination
when a medicine is injected into your body to stop you from getting a serious illness

van
a big machine with wheels that carries things from place to place

a red van

vegan
someone who does not eat anything that has come from an animal, including meat, milk, eggs and fish

Nancy is a vegan.

vacuum cleaner
a machine that cleans floors and carpets

vase
something you can fill with water and put flowers in

vegetable
part of a plant that you can eat.

Broccoli is a vegetable.

a b c d e f g h i j k l m n o p q r s t u v w x y z

101

a b c d e f g h i j k l m n o p q r s t u **v** w x y z

vegetarian

someone who does not eat meat or fish

Lee is a vegetarian.

very

a word you use before another one to make it stronger

The flashlight is very bright.

vet

someone who makes sure animals stay well and healthy

video

a short movie with movement and sound

Liz posted a video of herself singing.

view

all the things you can see from somewhere

violin

a musical instrument with strings

visit

go to see someone or something for a short time

Poppy is visiting her aunt.

visitor

someone who goes to a place to see someone or something for a short time

Aunt Dotty has visitors today.

voice

the sound you make when you talk or sing

Isaac has a lovely voice.

volcano

a mountain that sometimes spits out ash, gas and hot liquid rock called lava

vote

When you vote for someone, you show that you choose and support them.

Ww

wag
make something move from side to side

Daisy is wagging her tail.

wages
the money you earn by doing a job

I use my wages to buy food.

waist
the narrow part of your body, under your chest

Adam is pointing to his waist.

wait
stay in a place until something happens

Jill is waiting for her cake to cook.

wake (woke, woken)
stop sleeping and open your eyes

Lions often stretch when they wake up.

walk
move forwards by putting one foot in front of the other one

Ava is walking.

wall
1 one side of a room or building

This room has green walls.

2 something made of brick or stone that separates different areas of land

a brick wall

want
If you want something, you would like to have it.

Maria wants a new bike for her birthday.

a b c d e f g h i j k l m n o p q r s t u v **w** x y z

a b c d e f g h i j k l m n o p q r s t u v **w** x y z

warm

1 quite hot; not cold

a warm drink

2 If your clothes are warm, they will stop you from getting cold.

warm clothes

wash

make someone or something clean using soap and water

Zeb is washing his hands.

washing machine

a machine that washes clothes

wasp

a striped insect that can sting

watch¹

a small clock you wear on your wrist

watch²

keep looking at something for a while to see what happens

Lucas is watching birds.

water

the liquid in rivers and seas that falls as rain and comes out of a faucet

a glass of water

waterproof

Something waterproof keeps out water.

I'm glad my coat is waterproof.

wave¹

a hill of water that crashes on the shore

wave²

move your hand from side to side

Frankie is waving.

way¹

how you do something

This is the way you play the trumpet.

way[2]
how to get somewhere

Which is the way to the museum?

wear (wore, worn)
When you wear something, it covers part of your body.

Suzie is wearing blue boots.

weather
Weather is what it is like outside. There are many different kinds of weather. Here are some:

sunny   snowy

stormy   rainy

web
1 a thin net a spider makes to catch insects

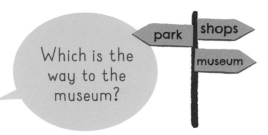

2 the part of the internet you use to find information

week
A week is 7 days. There are 52 weeks in a year.

weigh
find out how heavy someone or something is

We weighed the biggest pumpkin.

well[1]
healthy; not sick

Sam is well, but Paula is not.

well[2]
If you do something well, you are good at it.

Miguel draws very well.

wet
Something that is wet has water or another liquid on it.

This floor is wet.

whale
a huge animal that lives in the sea

a killer whale

a b c d e f g h i j k l m n o p q r s t u v **w** x y z

a b c d e f g h i j k l m n o p q r s t u v **w** x y z

wheel

a round thing that can turn around and around

a bicycle wheel

wheelchair

a chair on wheels that people who cannot always walk on their own use to move around

while

at the same time as something else is happening

Teri always sings while she's in the shower.

wide

measuring a lot from one side to the other; not narrow

a wide gate

wild

If animals or plants are wild, they are not looked after by people.

wild flowers

win (won, won)

come first in a race, game or competition

Fraser wins every year.

wind

air that moves around quickly outside

These leaves are blowing in the wind.

window

something in a wall or car that lets in light

Most windows are made of glass.

wing

the part of something that helps it to fly

Birds have two wings.

wish

really want something to happen, especially something not possible

I wish I could go outside.

with

1 If you are with someone, you are together.

I always walk home with Keely.

2 that has or who has

a dress with big spots

3 using

Kurt is playing with his toys.

woman (women)

a girl who has grown up

woman

girl

wood

1 the hard part of a tree that you can burn or make into things

2 a big group of trees growing close together

word

A word is a group of letters or sounds that mean something. You use words to speak, write or sing.

Hola

Bonjour

Hello

All these words mean "Hello."

work

1 do a job, usually for money

Penny works in an office.

2 If something works, it does what it is supposed to do.

Hurray! The lights work!

world

the planet we live on

This is what our world looks like from space.

a b c d e f g h i j k l m n o p q r s t u v **w** x y z

a b c d e f g h i j k l m n o p q r s t u v w **x** y z

write
(wrote, written)

use a pen, pencil, or a keyboard to put letters or words on something

Pat is writing a letter.

Dear

wrong
1 not correct or right

$$3 + 1 = 5$$

That's wrong!

2 behaving badly

It's wrong to drop trash.

Xx

x
1 the sign you use when you multiply in math

$$2 \times 2 = 4$$

2 what you write after your name if you want to send someone a kiss

Thank you! Love, Caroline x

x-ray

a kind of photograph that shows the inside of a part of someone's body

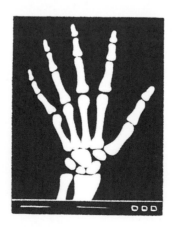

This is an x-ray of a hand.

xylophone

a musical instrument with a keyboard of wooden or metal bars

You hit the bars with sticks to play a xylophone.

Yy

yawn

open your mouth wide and breathe in deeply. You usually yawn when you are tired.

yet

up to this time

Oscar hasn't caught any fish yet.

young

If someone or something is young, they have not lived for a long time.

a young giraffe

year

A year is 12 months, from January to December.

yogurt

a creamy food made from milk

strawberry yogurt

Zz

zebra

an animal that looks like a horse with black and white stripes

zipper

something with metal or plastic teeth that you use to fasten clothes and bags

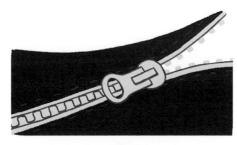

zoo

a place where animals are kept so that people can see them

a b c d e f g h i j k l m n o p q r s t u v w x y z

Words we use a lot

On these pages, you'll find words that aren't in the main part of the dictionary, but are very useful when you're reading or writing.

a
about
above
across
again
all
almost
also
always
am
among
an
and
another
anybody
anyone
anything
anywhere
apart
are
around

as
at
away

be
because
but
by

can
can't
could
couldn't

each
every
everybody
everyone
everything
everywhere

for
from

get
got

he
he'd
he'll
her
here
hers
herself
he's
him
himself
his
how

I
I'd
if
I'll
I'm
in
into

is
isn't
it
its
it's
itself

just

may
me
might
mine
must
my
myself

no
nobody
none
no one
not
nothing
nowhere

of	than	tomorrow	who
off	that	too	whose
on	the		why
or	their	unless	will
our	theirs	until	won't
ours	them	up	would
ourselves	themselves	upon	wouldn't
out	then	us	
	there		yes
she	these	we	yesterday
she'd	they	we'd	you
she'll	they'd	we'll	you'd
she's	they'll	were	you'll
should	they're	we're	your
so	this	what	you're
some	those	when	yours
somebody	to	where	yourself
someone	today	which	yourselves
something			
sometimes			
somewhere			

This list will really help me with my spelling.

Numbers

1	one	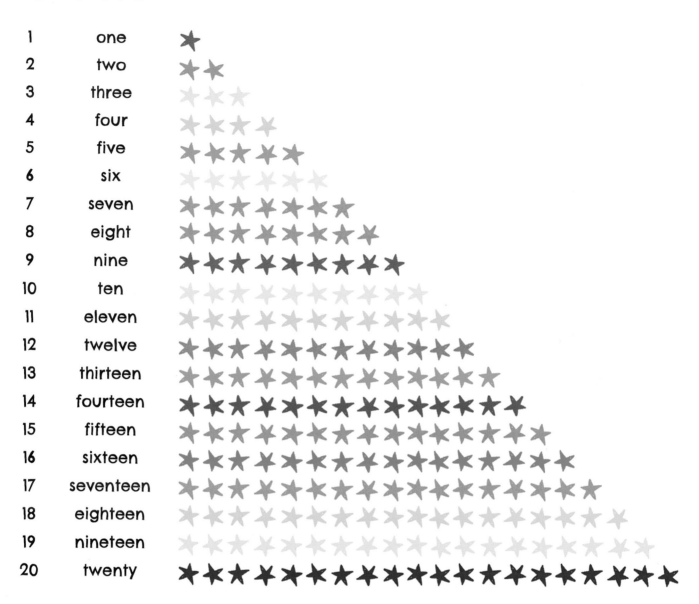
2	two	
3	three	
4	four	
5	five	
6	six	
7	seven	
8	eight	
9	nine	
10	ten	
11	eleven	
12	twelve	
13	thirteen	
14	fourteen	
15	fifteen	
16	sixteen	
17	seventeen	
18	eighteen	
19	nineteen	
20	twenty	

Days of the week

These five days are **weekdays.**

These days are the **weekend.**

Monday	Tuesday	Wednesday	Thursday	Friday	Saturday	Sunday

Months of the year

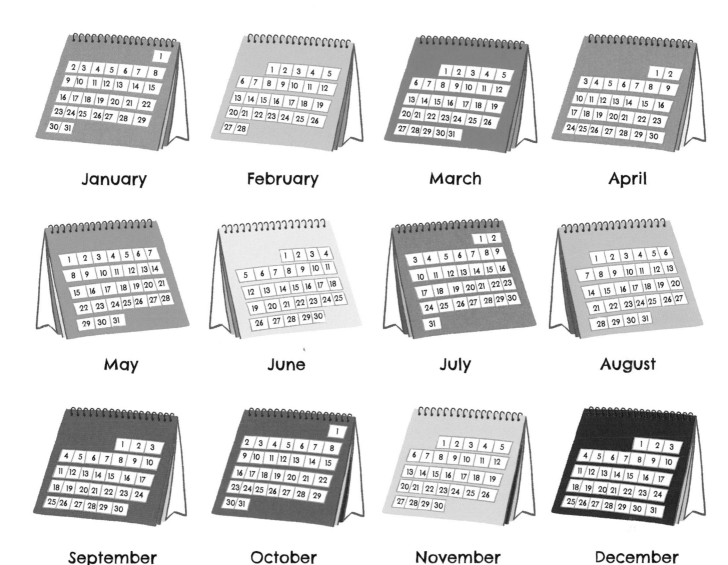

January   February   March   April

May   June   July   August

September   October   November   December

Seasons

spring   summer   fall   winter

Colors

red

white

orange

brown

yellow

purple

pink

green

blue

black

These are just a few colors, but there are lots more!

Shapes

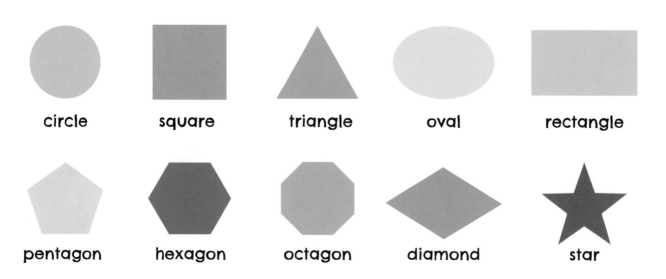

circle

square

triangle

oval

rectangle

pentagon

hexagon

octagon

diamond

star

Family words

This is Joe's family. Let's find out who's who in it.

Joe and Theo are our **sons** and Lily is our **daughter.**

I'm Joe's **cousin.** My name's Arlo.

Joe, Theo and Arlo are our **grandsons** and Lily is our **granddaughter.**

Joe

Lily

Theo

Joe has a big **sister** named Lily and a little **brother** named Theo.

Here are Joe's **parents,** Matt and Anna. Joe calls them "Mom" and "Dad."

This is Anna's sister Eve. She is Joe's **aunt** and her husband Sean is his **uncle.**

Anna's parents live with the family. They are Joe's **grandparents.**

Feelings

People feel lots of different things, so there are many words you can use to describe feelings. Some are in this dictionary, such as "happy," "angry" and "sad," but here are some more you could use to describe how you feel.

How are YOU feeling today?

mad   worried   excited   confused   curious   overjoyed

Habitats

Different kinds of animals and plants need different things to survive. Each kind has its own habitat, which is the name for the place which provides them with what they need. Here are some important habitats around the world.

deserts

mountains

woods and forests

oceans

rainforests

polar regions

Story words

These words are often found in stories about magical creatures and imaginary places. You could use them in your writing, too.

dragon

castle

desert island

fairy

elf
fairy
giant
goblin
legend
monster
ogre
prince
princess
spell
witch
wizard

What kinds of words?

There are four main kinds of words in English, and each one does a different job. They are called verbs, nouns, adjectives and adverbs. You'll find out more about them and how to use them on these pages.

These are the four main kinds of words and the jobs that they do.

verb

a doing or action word

Jack is <u>jumping</u>.

"Jump" is a verb.

noun

a thing or an object

a beautiful <u>butterfly</u>

adjective

a word that describes something

a <u>tiny</u> ant

adverb

a word that tells you how something is done

Albie played the drums <u>well</u>.

"Well" is an adverb.

The sentence below uses one of each word type. Can you spot the verb, noun, adjective and adverb?

The new choir sang loudly.

Check your answers on the last page.

How words change

Words can change according to what you want them to mean. Here are some things you might need to know about verbs, adjectives and nouns.

Talking about the past

Verbs, or "doing words," change when you use them to talk about the past (the time before now). Usually, you just add "ed" or "d" to the end of the verb, like this:

Mia <u>dances</u> very well.

Yesterday, Mia <u>danced</u> with Sergio.

Mia has <u>danced</u> with Sergio every day this week.

For some verbs, you don't add those endings but change the word in other ways when you are talking about the past:

Adam <u>hides</u> when it's time for bed.

Yesterday, he <u>hid</u> for more than an hour.

A few times, he has <u>hidden</u> for so long that he's fallen asleep.

In this dictionary, you can see how these verbs change in parentheses ( ), like this:

give (gave, given)
let someone have something
Chloe gave Josh her old bike.

118

Comparing things

You can use describing words, or adjectives, to compare things as well as to describe them. Usually, you just add "er" or "est" to the end of the adjective:

A cat is small<u>er</u> than a dog,

... but a mouse is the small<u>est</u> of all.

Squeak!

Sometimes, you add "more" or "most" <u>before</u> the adjective to compare things:

This ring is expensive.

This necklace is <u>more</u> expensive.

This crown is <u>the most</u> expensive.

For a few adjectives, the whole word changes when comparing things:

This picture is <u>good</u>.

This picture is <u>better</u>.

This picture is <u>best</u>.

In this dictionary, you'll find any unusual changes in parentheses ( ) after the word: —

good (better, best)
1 If something is good, you like it.

This book is the best!

More than one

Nouns (naming words) usually change when you use them to talk about more than one thing, and they can change in several different ways.

For most nouns, you just add an "s" onto the end of the word:

one apple   two apple<u>s</u>

If the noun already ends in an "s," you add "es," so "dress" becomes "dresses":

one dress   two dress<u>es</u>

A few nouns have a different ending when there's more than one:

one child   two child<u>ren</u>

Some nouns change completely!

one <u>mouse</u>   two <u>mice</u>

And a very few don't change at all.

one <u>sheep</u>   two <u>sheep</u>   three <u>sheep</u>

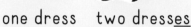

If there's an unusual change, you'll find it in parentheses after a word to remind you.

child (children)
a young person
two children

p117 answers: The new choir sang loudly: "new" is an adjective; "choir" is a noun; "sang" is a verb; "loudly" is an adverb.

Additional artworking by Keith Newell   Additional design by Matthew Durber
With thanks to Jane Bingham, Holly Bathie, Jessica Greenwell and Kristie Pickersgill
Americanization by Carrie Armstrong